SCHIRMER'S LIBRARY
OF MUSICAL CLASSICS

Compositions for the Piano
FRÉDÉRIC CHOPIN

Edited, Revised, and Fingered by
RAFAEL JOSEFFY

Historical and Analytical Comments by
JAMES HUNEKER

G. SCHIRMER, Inc.

DISTRIBUTED BY

HAL•LEONARD®
CORPORATION

7777 W. BLUEMOUND RD. P.O. BOX 13819 MILWAUKEE, WI 53213

FOUR SCHERZI AND FANTASY

FRÉDÉRIC Chopin bequeathed to the world of music six solo Scherzi. The four that comprise a group are opus 20, in B minor, published February, 1835; opus 31, in B flat minor, published December, 1837; opus 39, in C sharp minor, published October, 1840; and opus 54, in E major, published December, 1843. The remaining two Scherzi are to be found in his second Sonata, opus 35, and third Sonata, opus 58, and are discussed in the volume devoted to the Three Sonatas. These six compositions are most striking evidences of Chopin's originality, power and delicacy. The Scherzo, however, is not his invention. Beethoven and Mendelssohn anticipated him. But he took the form, remodelled and filled it with a surprisingly novel content, though not altering its three-four measure. In Beethoven we feel the humor of his Scherzo, its swing, its robustness, its rude jollity. One enjoys the lightness, velocity and finish of Mendelssohn's *scherzando* moods; strictly speaking, they contain more of the true Scherzo idea than Chopin's. Mendelssohn's sentiment of refined joyousness stems from Scarlatti and other early Italian masters of the piano. They are full of a certain gracious life, a surface-skimming of sentiment like the curved flight of birds over shallow waters. But we enter a different, a terrible, a beautiful domain in the Chopin Scherzi. Two only have the clarity of atmosphere, lightness of touch, and sweet gayety of the veritable Scherzo; the others are grave, fierce, sardonic, demoniacal, ironic, passionate, hysterical and most melancholy. In some the mood seems pathologic; in some enigmatic; in all the mood is magical. These four Scherzi are psychical records, confessions committed to paper of outpourings that never could have passed the lips. From these we may reconstruct the inner Chopin, whose well-bred exterior so ill prepared the world for the tragic issues of his music.

The first Scherzo in B minor is in his most sombre, ironic and reckless vein; Chopin throwing himself to the very winds of remorse. A self-torturing, a Manfred mood. Structurally speaking it is a fair model for the others: a few bars of introduction—the porch, as Niecks would call it—a principal subject, a trio, a short working-out section, a skillful return to the opening theme and an elaborate *coda*. Some pianists play the piece without the repeats and it is the gainer thereby, as the *da capo* is unsuited to latter-day taste. The architecture, not technically flawless, is better adapted to the florid musical beauties of the Byzantine than to the severer Hellenic line. The arabesque-like figure after the eight-bar introduction—muted bars some of them, as is Chopin's wont—bears a certain spiritual likeness to the principal figure in the Fantaisie-Impromptu. But instead of the ductile triplets, as in the bass of the Impromptu, the figure in the Scherzo is divided between two hands, and the harshness of the mood is emphasized by the anticipatory chord in the left hand. The vitality of the first page is remarkable. The questioning chords at the close of the section are as imaginative as any Chopin wrote. The half-notes and up-leaping *appoggiatura* testify to his originality in details; these occur before the modulation into the lyric theme in B, and with a slight change at the dash into the *coda*. The second section, *agitato*, contains some knotty harmonic problems; it must be taken at a tempestuous speed, else cacophony. Chopin here is bold to excess. The *molto più lento* is a masterpiece; it is written in the luscious key of B major and is a woven tonal enchantment. It is only comparable to the B major episode in the B minor Étude for octaves, or to the Tuberose Nocturne in B major. Mark how the composer returns to his first savage mood. It is a picture of contrasted violence. The *coda* is like an electrifying cross-country ride, barbaric in its impetuosity. The heavy accentuation on the first note of every bar should not blind one's rhythmic sense to the second beat in the left hand, which is likewise accented. These mixed rhythms add to the general despair of the *finale*. The shrill dissonances, so logical, so effective, must have lacerated the eardrums of Chopin's contemporaries. And they must be vigorously insisted upon. I think it was Tausig who first taught his pupils to use the interlocked octaves at the close instead of the chromatic scales in unison, though I suppose Liszt did it before any one else; he always thought of such things, even when the composer did not. Chopin, however, probably objected to the innovation, which may be admissible. Coming after the Hercules-vein of the *coda* the plain scales sound a trifle thin and tame. This Scherzo has been criticised as being too much in the étude style, but that depends very much upon the pianist who plays it. When Rubinstein sat in front of the keyboard it became in his hands a tornado of wrathful mutterings and outcries. It was his favorite.

We are on more familiar footing in the second Scherzo in B flat minor. Who has not heard with a certain awe those arched questioning triplets, which Chopin never could get his pupils to play sufficiently *tombé!* "It must be a charnel-house," he told De Lenz. But those vaulted phrases have since become banal. Alas! This Scherzo, like the lovely A flat Ballade, has been done to death. Yet, how fresh, how vigorous, how abounding in sweetness and light is this music when it falls from the hands of a master. It is then a Byronic poem, "So tender, so bold, so full of love, as of scorn"—to quote Schumann. Chopin never penned a more delicious song than the trio. The section in A is serious to severity, yet how penetrating is its perfume. The excursion into C sharp minor may be the awakening of the wondering dream; but it is balanced, with no suggestions of the pallid morbidities of the other Chopin. Style and theme are perfectly welded. It all lies in the very heart of the piano. Fearful that he has dwelt too long upon the idea, the composer breaks away and follows a burst into the clear sky. After the repetition comes the working-out section, and though ingenious and effective, it is always in development that Chopin is weakest. The Olympian aloofness of Beethoven he has not; he cannot survey his material from an objective viewpoint. He is a great composer, but he is also a great pianist. He nursed his ideas with constructive frugality, but the instrument often checked his imagination. There is logic in the exposition of this Scherzo, but it is piano-logic, not always music-logic. A certain straining after brilliancy, a falling off in the spontaneous urge of the early pages force us to feel happier when the first triplet figure returns. The *coda* is strong. This Scherzo will remain the favored one. It is not cryptic or repellent like the two examples in B minor and C sharp minor, and therefore is a perennial joy to pupil, teacher and public. Yet it is not as logical, as profound, as the first and third Scherzi.

The third Scherzo in C sharp minor was composed, or else finished, at Majorca. It is the most dramatic of this set. Irony lurks in its polished phrases and there is fever and seething scorn. The work is clear-cut and of exact balance. Chopin founded whole paragraphs either on a single phrase repeated in similar shapes or on two phrases in alternation—a primitive practice in Polish folksong. Hadow asserts that "Beethoven does not attain the lucidity of his style by such parallelism of phraseology," and admits that Chopin's methods made for "clearness and precision . . . and may be regarded as a characteristic of the national manner." A thoroughly personal characteristic, too. There is virile clangor on the firmly struck octaves of the opening page—no hesitating, morbid view of life, but harsh assertiveness, not untinged with splenetic anger. The chorale of the trio is admirably devised and carried out, though its piety may well be a bit of liturgical make-believe. Here the contrasts are most artistic—sonorous harmonies set off by broken chords that deliciously tinkle. There is a frenetic *coda* and the close in the major

is surprising considering what has preceded it. Never to become the property of the profane, the C sharp minor Scherzo, notwithstanding its marked asperity of mood, is a supreme art in its particular province. Without the inner freedom of its predecessors, it is more self-contained than the B minor Scherzo. But it is a sombre and fantastic pile of architecture, and about it hovers despairing and perpetual night. It is a tale from Poe's "iron-bound, melancholy volume of the magi,'" and on its gates might be inscribed the word Spleen. De Lenz relates that Chopin dedicated the work to his pupil Gutmann, because this giant, with the fist of a prize-fighter, could "knock a hole in the table" with a certain chord for the left hand—sixth measure from the beginning—and adds quite naïvely: "Nothing more was ever heard of Gutmann —he was a discovery of Chopin's." Chopin died in this same Gutmann's arms, and, despite De Lenz, Gutmann was, until the death of the master, a "favorite pupil."

The fourth Scherzo in E may be described by no better word than delightful. It is sunny music, and its swiftness, sweep, and directness are compelling. The five preluding bars of half-notes, *unisono*, strike at once the keynote of optimism. What follows is like the ruffling of tree-tops by warm south winds. The upward little flight in E, beginning at the seventeenth bar, and in major thirds and fourths, has been happily utilized by Saint-Saëns in the Scherzo of his G minor piano concerto. The fanciful embroidery of the single finger passages is crystalline in clarity. A sparkling freedom and bubbling freshness characterize this Scherzo, too seldom heard in concert recitals. It is not in emotional content deep; it lies well within the categories of the capricious and elegant. On its fourth page it contains an episode in E which at first blush suggests the theme of the Waltz in A flat, opus 42, with its interminglements of duple and triple rhythms. The *più lento* further on has a touch of sadness; it is but the blur of a passing cloud that shadows with its fleecy edges the wind-swept moorland. The prevailing mood is one of joyousness; as joyous as the witty, sensitive Pole ever allowed himself to be. Its *coda* is not as forceful as the usual Chopin *coda*, and there is a dazzling flutter of silvery scale at the end. It is a charming work, a jesting of a superior sort. Niecks thinks it fragmentary. I find the fairy-like mood a relief after the doleful message of the earlier Scherzi. There is the same "spirit of opposition"; of sneering arrogance, none. Yet the composition seems to be banned by both classicists and Chopin-worshippers.

Robert Schumann, after remarking that the cosmopolitan must "sacrifice the small interests of the soil on which he was born," notes that the later works of Chopin "begin to lose something of their essential Sarmatian physiognomy, to approach partly the universal ideal cultivated by the divine Greeks, which we find again in Mozart." The F minor Fantasy, opus 49, has hardly the Mozartian serenity, yet it parades a formal beauty, not disfigured by excess of violence, either personal or patriotic, and its melodies, though restless and melancholy, are of surpassing nobility and dramatic grandeur. I do not fear to maintain that this Fantasy is one of the greatest among piano pieces. After more than a half-century of neglect it has at last been given its due position in the pianists' pantheon. For Niecks, who did not at first discern its worth, it suggests a Titan in commotion. It is titanic, the torso of some Faust-like dream. It is Chopin's Faust. A *macabre* march, containing some dangerous dissonances, gravely ushers us to ascending staircases of triplets, only to precipitate us into the very abysses of the piano bass. The first subject, is is not as puissant and as passionate as if Beethoven had written it? But Chopin's lack of tenaciousness is soon apparent. Beethoven would have built a tonal cathedral on such a foundational scheme; but Chopin, ever prodigal in his melody-making, impetuously dashes on to the A flat episode, that heroic love-chant, so often played with the effeminacies of the salon. Its reappearance in various keys, the peaceful *Lento Sostenuto* in B and conclusion are alike masterly.

Vladimir de Pachmann avers that Franz Liszt told him the programme of this Fantasy, according to Chopin. At the close of one immemorial day the composer was at the piano, his spirits vastly depressed. Suddenly came a knocking at the door, a Poe-like, sinister tapping which he at once rhythmically echoed upon the keyboard. The first two bars of the Fantasy describe these rappings, just as the third and fourth stand for Chopin's musical in-vitation, *entrez! entrez!* All this repeated till the doors swinging wide admit George Sand, Liszt, Madame Camille Pleyel (*née* Mock) and others of the Chopin group. To the solemn measures of the march they enter and range themselves about the pianist, who, after the agitated triplets, begins his complaint in the mysterious F minor song. But Madame Sand, with whom he had quarrelled, falls before him on her knees and pleads for pardon. Straightway the chant merges into the appealing A flat section, and from the C minor the current becomes more tempestuous until the climax is reached, and to the second march (which for me always has a Schumannesque tinge) the intruders rapidly vanish. This far from ideal reading may be an authoritative one, coming as it does from Chopin by way of Liszt. I console myself for its rather commonplace character with the notion that, perhaps, in its retelling, the story has caught some personal cadenzas of the two historians.

Chopin had never before so artistically maintained such an exalted passion, displayed such intellectual power or kept to such a euphonious level, as in the F minor Fantasy. It is his largest canvas, the phraseology is broad and long-breathed, and there is no padding of paragraphs. The virtuoso makes way for the poet. The interest is not relaxed until the final bar. This big work approaches Beethoven in its unity, in theme, mood, formal rectitude and economy of thematic material. I am loath to believe that the echo of its magical music will ever fall upon unheeding ears.

James Huneker

Thematic Index

Scherzos and Fantaisie

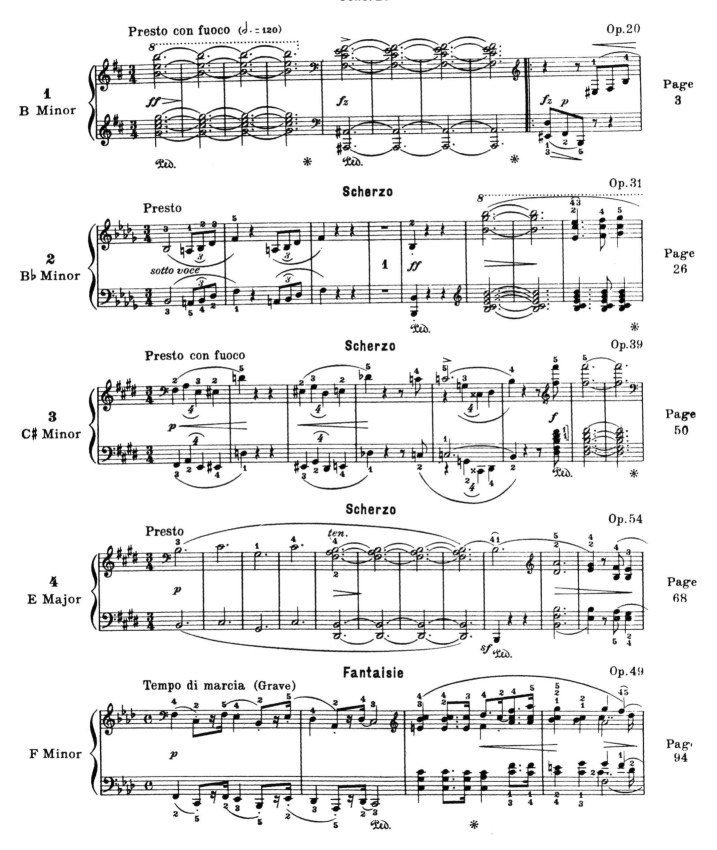

à Mr. F. Albrecht

Scherzo

Edited and fingered by
Rafael Joseffy

F. Chopin. Op. 20

25489 x

sempre più animato

12

25489

(a) Klindworth:

14

Molto più lento (♩=108)

sotto voce legato

ritenuto   *a tempo*   *poco a poco cresc.*

con anima

(a) **Probably for the sake of clearness, Klindworth indicates the melody in the following manner**

25489

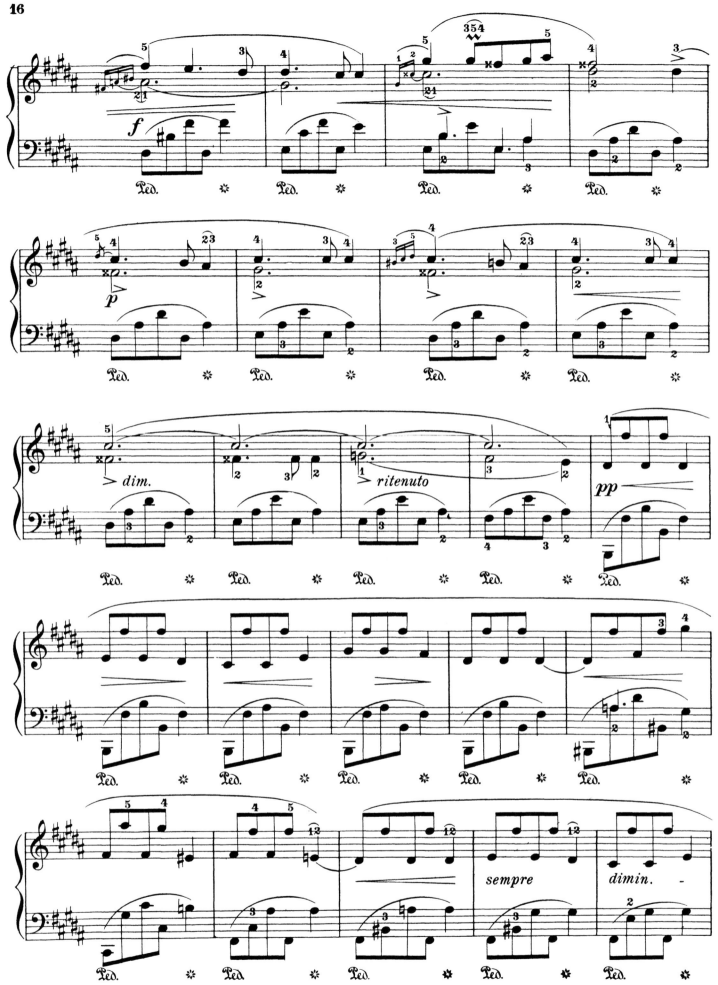

risoluto e sempre più animato

à Mlle. la Comtesse de Fürstenstein

Scherzo

Edited and fingered by
Rafael Joseffy

F. Chopin. Op. 31

25489

Copyright, 1915, by G. Schirmer, Inc.

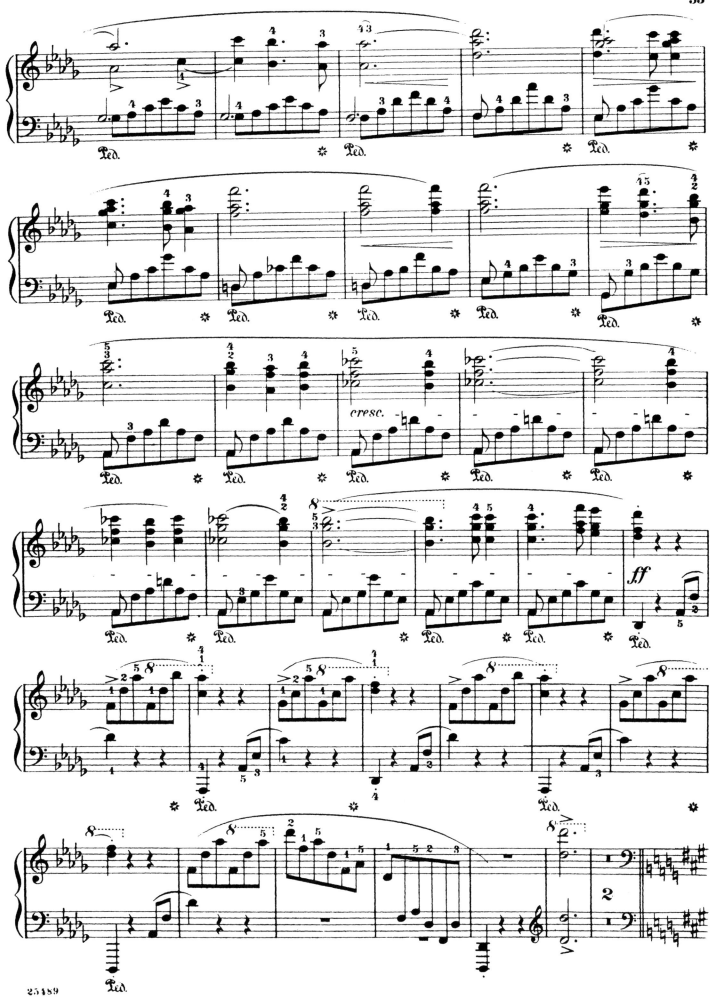

25489

38

25489

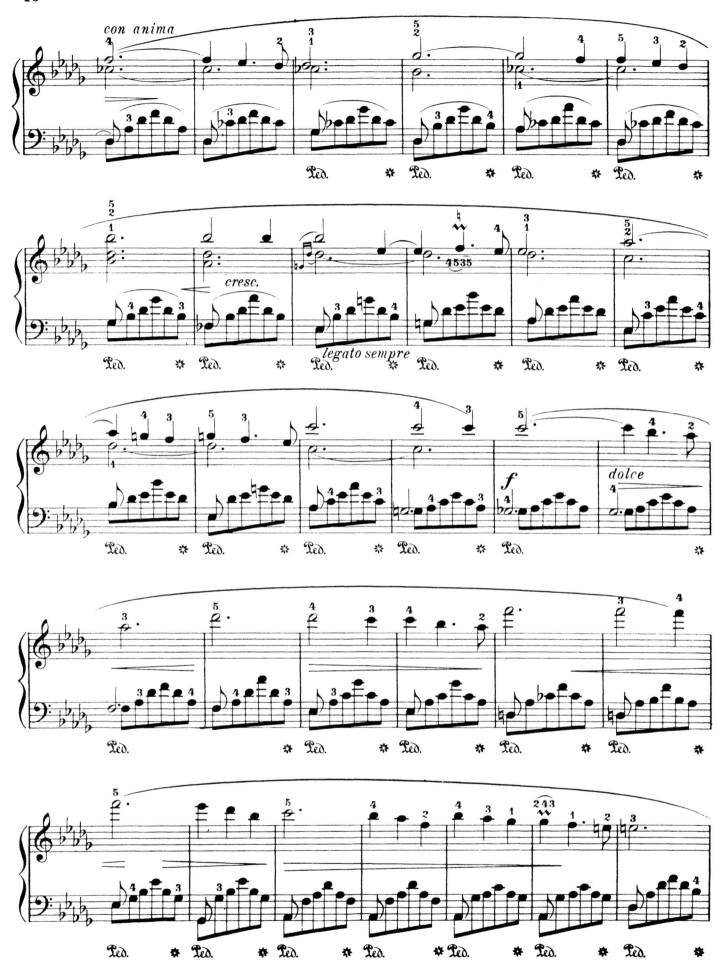

à Mr. A. Gutman

Scherzo

Edited and fingered by
Rafael Joseffy

F. Chopin. Op. 39

Presto con fuoco

Risoluto

25489

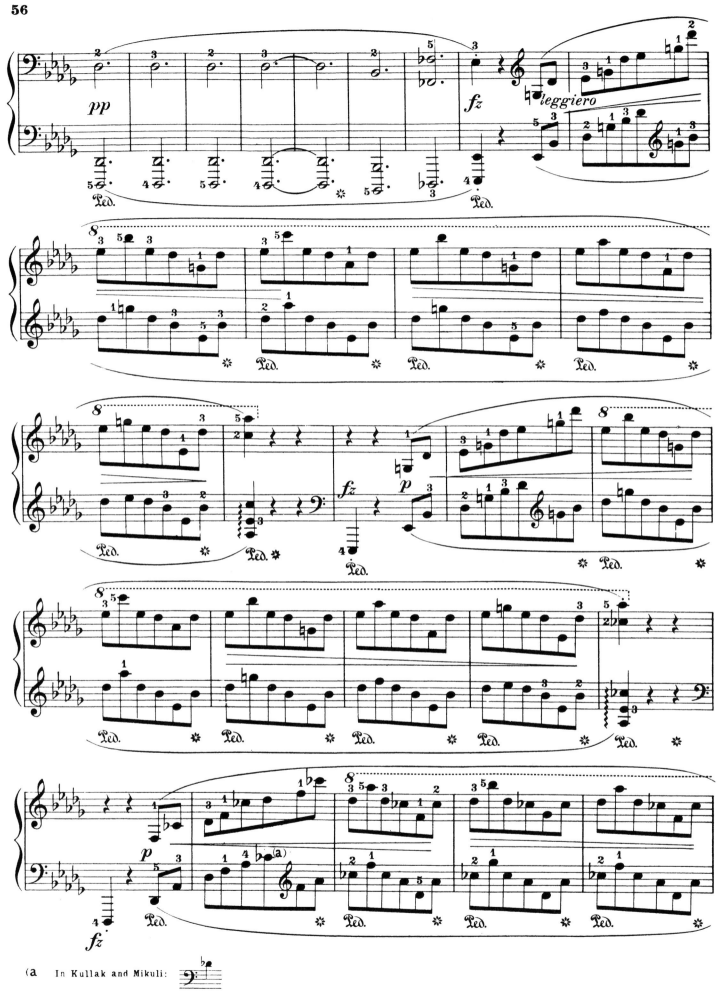

(a   In Kullak and Mikuli:

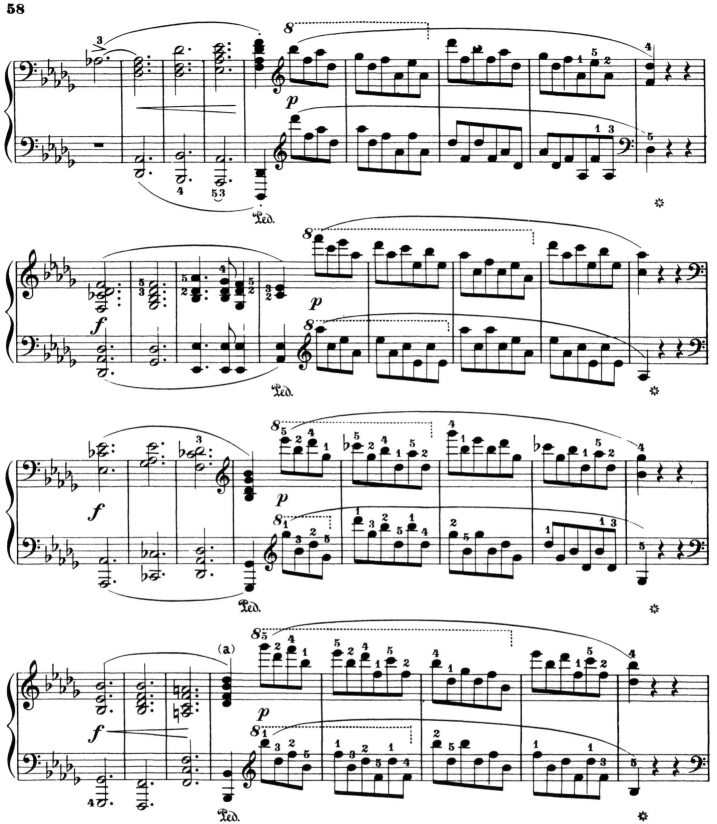

(a) Formerly, and in the Original Edition

Tempo I°

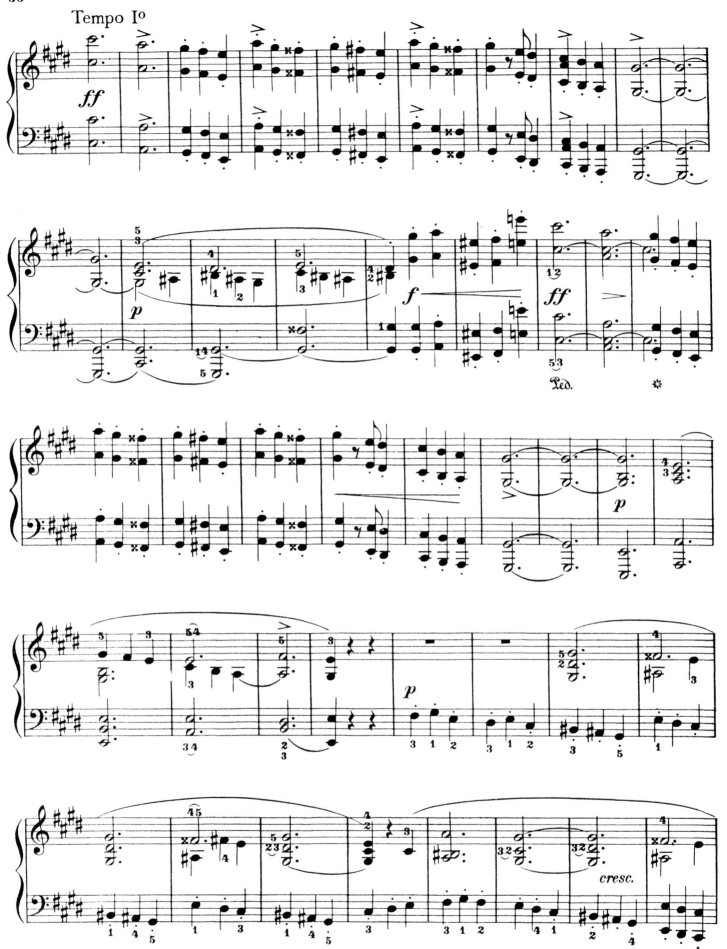

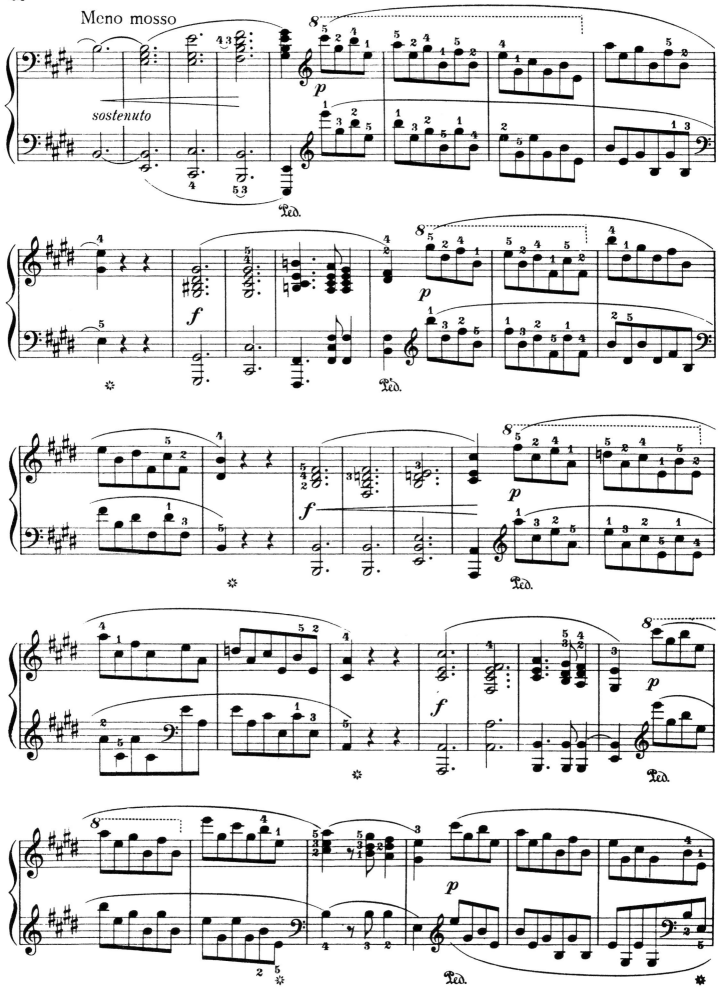

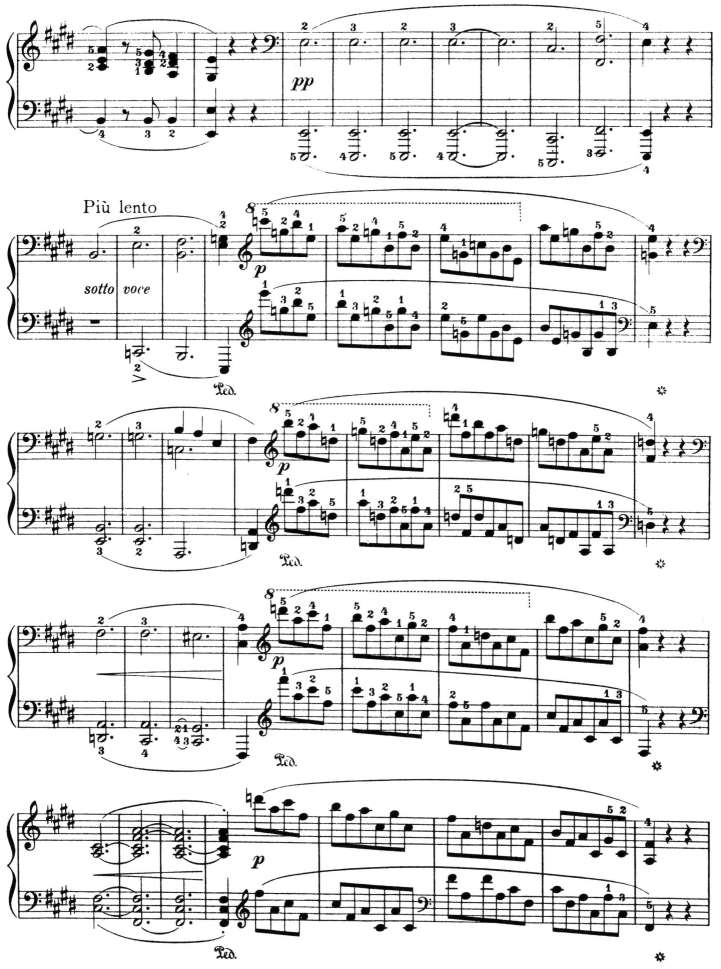

Edited and fingered by
Rafael Joseffy

à Mlle. Clotilde de Caraman

Scherzo

F. Chopin. Op. 54

25489

25489

decresc. ed accel.

Tempo Io
in tempo

cresc.

(a) Klindworth Edition: *decresc. e poco rallent.(al tempo primo)*

25489

88

25489

à Mme. la Princesse Cath. de Souzzo

Fantaisie

Edited and fingered by
Rafael Joseffy

F. Chopin. Op. 49

Tempo di marcia (Grave)

Copyright, 1915, by G. Schirmer, Inc.

25489

(a) Klindworth's notation:

etc.

(a) Klindworth:

Lento sostenuto

(a) Klindworth's notation:

etc.

Più mosso

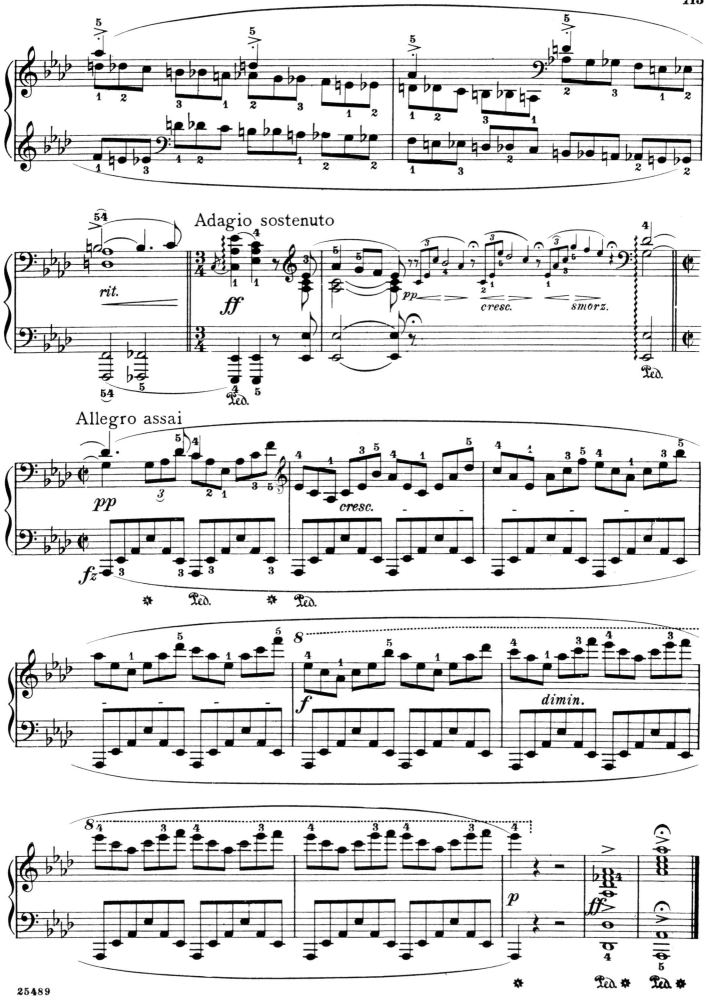